THE GIANTS OF COMEDY™

KATE MCKINNON

C. R. MCKAY

Rosen YA™

New York

Published in 2020 by The Rosen Publishing Group, Inc.
29 East 21st Street, New York, NY 10010

First Edition

Library of Congress Cataloging-in-Publication Data

Names: McKay, C. R. (Writer of juvenile fiction), author.
Title: Kate McKinnon / C.R. McKay.
Description: First edition. | New York : Rosen Publishing, 2020. | Series: The giants of comedy | Audience: Grades 7–12. | Includes bibliographical references and index.
Identifiers: LCCN 2018048744| ISBN 9781508188674 (library bound) | ISBN 9781508188667 (paperback)
Subjects: LCSH: McKinnon, Kate, 1984– —Juvenile literature. | Women comedians—United States—Biography—Juvenile literature.
Classification: LCC PN2287.M5464 M35 2020 | DDC 791.4302/8092 [B] —dc23
LC record available at https://lccn.loc.gov/2018048744

Manufactured in China

On the cover: As shown here at the 2017 Emmy Awards, Kate McKinnon is almost always seen with a big grin and a quick wit.

CONTENTS

Introduction

What is it like to work for a laugh? What is it like to impersonate someone on stage? What is it like to write satire that affects how people view anything from celebrity behavior to politics? Look no further than the master of comedic satire and laugh-out-loud impressions: Kate McKinnon.

Kate McKinnon shot to fame for her spot-on impressions and smart, goofy humor. McKinnon is a comedian who is not afraid to get a little weird or act so over-the-top that one wonders how she can even keep a straight face. Alex Morris of *Rolling Stone* magazine even dubbed McKinnon the "*SNL* Weirdo in Chief" for her work on America's most popular late-night sketch show, *Saturday Night Live* (*SNL*).

McKinnon has won the hearts of people across the United States, taking home two Emmys for Outstanding Supporting Actress in a Comedy Series for her work on *SNL* in both 2016 and 2017. She won the Critics' Choice TV Award for Best Actress

Kate McKinnon has never been afraid to act crazy, goofy, or silly to get a laugh—and she has gotten very good at doing so.

in a Comedy Series in 2016, as well as the Dorian Award from the Gay and Lesbian Entertainment Critics Association. McKinnon has broken barriers as the first openly gay female member of *SNL* and inspires many with her ability to be so openly true to herself.

McKinnon made her debut on the big screen in the 2016 remake of *Ghostbusters*. She is also a voice actor, playing the role of Ms. Frizzle in the 2017 reboot of the *Magic School Bus* series, Squeaks in the educational TV series *Nature Cat*, and Lupe in the movie *Ferdinand*.

Apart from comedy and acting, McKinnon is in a world of her own. She is constantly learning and trying new things, including how to rap in Hungarian. She is a self-proclaimed astrophysics nerd who loves science. She is also crazy for cooking and her rescue cat, Nino. McKinnon's interests are about as varied, bright, and unique as her comedic and fashion styles.

Despite having a loud and offbeat personality on stage and in movies, McKinnon is actually a very private person. While many comedians have written books about their lives, McKinnon is generally quiet about her personal life. Where most public figures today are on every social media platform, from Instagram to Twitter, McKinnon has no accounts. In a roundtable interview with Stacey Wilson Hunt and Michael O'Connell of *Hollywood Reporter*, McKinnon joked, "If I had Instagram, it would be pictures of my son, who is a cat. That's mostly what's going on with me."

When asked how she is able to play so many wild characters with such a private personality, McKinnon says that acting is her way of reaching out. She told Dave Itzkoff of the *New York Times*, "That's the way I feel most comfortable connecting."

Even though McKinnon lives a life of fame and high-profile comedy now, she had very simple beginnings. She often talks about her gratitude for being able to work as much as she does and told Hunt and O'Connell of *Hollywood Reporter* that she'd even work "for a hamburger." In her signature serious-yet-goofy way, she clarifies, "I just want to be onstage. And I want a hamburger."

Kate McKinnon's story is a reminder that working as a comedian is not always glamorous or a straight road. However, she has rolled up her sleeves to achieve success and is now known as one of the hardest working comedy writers and performers in the United States.

CHAPTER
ONE

A Funny Beginning

Kate McKinnon is a New Yorker through and through. She grew up in the town of Sea Cliff on Long Island, New York. Born on January 6, 1984, her full name is Kathryn McKinnon Berthold.

McKinnon's mother, Laura, was a social worker and her father, Michael, was an architect. While they held normal, everyday jobs, Kate came from a household of comedy lovers. Her mother was a public speaker and had been the president of her high school's drama club. Her father enjoyed comedy and encouraged Kate to watch as much of it as possible.

McKinnon told Lili Anolik of *Vanity Fair* that her family watched *The Producers* once a week. Her family loved movies and television shows from classic comedy writers and producers. In an interview with Leigh Flayton of Refinery 29, McKinnon said of her parents, "There was a lot of sketch comedy in the house. They loved *SNL*.

The Berthold family was no stranger to comedy. Mel Brooks's 1967 classic film *The Producers* was one of Kate McKinnon's earliest comedic inspirations.

They encouraged us to watch Mel Brooks movies, which was required viewing."

Funny Runs in the Family

McKinnon is not the only one in her family to go into comedy. Her sister, Emily Lynne, is a stand-up comedian. With a similar voice and movements—not to mention a knack for getting laughs—the resemblance between Emily and Kate is obvious.

Kate and Emily have been performing together since they were kids. They produced funny videos together, making up ridiculous characters—perhaps Kate's first step into satire and impersonations. Kate remembers watching comedy movies over and over, learning all the dialogue. Their favorite movies included *Troop Beverly Hills* and *Legally Blonde.* In 2015, Kate and Emily appeared together in a web series titled *Notary Publix*, just one of the many collaborations in their lives.

With a passion for performance and comedy, McKinnon was not a cookie-cutter kid. She loved to dress up and do different funny voices. She often went to school in costume, whether it was Peter Pan or Pippi Longstocking. She loved being able to dress up and be someone new each Halloween. Even then, she was creating characters, doing impressions, and growing in her comedy.

Legally Blonde is a 2001 comedy film starring Reese Witherspoon about a sorority girl who decides to go to Harvard Law School; it is a McKinnon favorite.

McKinnon was a naturally artistic child. She also did very well in school and loved to perform for people. She learned to play several instruments, including the cello, guitar, and piano. She played piano from the age of five and picked up the guitar and cello in middle school.

A COMEDIAN AND A MUSICIAN

Kate McKinnon's musical training as a child has often been incorporated into her performances. One of her most memorable sketches on *SNL* happened after the 2016 election. Hillary Clinton had just lost the presidential race to Donald Trump. For many people in the country, this was a shocking defeat.

In the November 12, 2016, episode of *SNL*, McKinnon—who was a strong supporter of Hillary Clinton—dressed as the politician, as she had for months on the show. Then, she played the song "Hallelujah" by Leonard Cohen, who had just died that week. McKinnon belted out the verses of the classic song, while playing the piano during the live show. When she finished, she looked at the camera and said, "I'm not giving up, and neither should you." It was a significant moment for McKinnon, for the show, and for the country.

Comedy and Tragedy

As much as McKinnon loved music, though, there was one thing she could not get enough of: comedy. "I've been doing funny voices since I was five. It's always been the way I communicated most comfortably with the rest of the world," she told Yelena Shuster of *Columbia College Today*.

McKinnon can remember the exact moment she really caught the comedy bug. She told Alex Morris of *Rolling Stone* that her first real taste of being a comedian happened in fifth grade. She used a British accent in her audition to be the "queen of reading week" and found her talent. She said, "I think the genesis of my entire life, probably, was the smiles I elicited doing this British accent. I've been chasing that dragon ever since."

Unfortunately, when Kate was only eighteen years old, her father—one of her biggest comedic influences—died. He had been battling brain cancer for several years, which was both emotionally and financially draining for the entire family.

McKinnon remembered her father when she won her Emmy, dedicating the award to him. In her acceptance speech, she said, "On a personal note, thank you to my beautiful and hilarious mother and sister and to my father, who's not with us anymore, but he made me start watching *SNL* when I was twelve, so thank you, and I miss you, Pop." Though he passed when she was young, McKinnon keeps his memory alive every time she cracks a joke or does an impression.

Despite the rough years of her father's illness, McKinnon still kept her dream alive. She also kept alive her love for comedy, which she had shared with her father. She set her eyes on theater, performing in recitals and plays. Her hard work and determination paid off—she was admitted to the Columbia University theater program after high school.

THE SKETCHES THAT KEEP YOU IN STITCHES

Saturday Night Live is the most popular late night sketch comedy show in the world. Sketch comedy is a form of comedy that involves short scenes that range from around one to ten minutes long. They are normally rehearsed ahead of time and then performed live for an audience. *SNL* has millions of

Saturday Night Live launched the careers of many of the most famous comedians of the twentieth century, including Bill Murray, Chevy Chase, and Gilda Radner, among many others.

viewers who tune in each Saturday to see what the comedians will do next.

The show got its start in 1975 and has since had a huge impact on comedy, both past and present. Many famous comedians and actors, including Tina Fey, Amy Poehler, Chris Rock, Jimmy Fallon, and Will Ferrell, got their start on this late-night show. The show has won sixty-four Emmys as of 2018. It continues to shape not only the comedy of today, but also the politics. Sketches often touch on political subjects and mirror the feelings and concerns of people around the United States and the world.

Finding Comedy in College

Columbia University's theater program ranks among some of the best in the United States. Located in New York City, it is a hub for culture, both comedic and otherwise. Many actors move to New York City for acting opportunities both onstage and onscreen. Students have the opportunity to learn by doing, producing and acting in plays and performances

Columbia University was founded in 1754 in New York City. Its long history makes it well known around the world for its excellence, and McKinnon was drawn to its prestigious theater program after high school.

throughout their college career. They are able to learn from famous guest lecturers, actors who are successful in their field.

McKinnon made the most of her time at Columbia University, where she was known by her given name, Kate Berthold. It was here that she started to make a reputation for herself in the world of satirical comedy for her part in the Varsity Show. The university calls its Varsity Show "Columbia's oldest performing arts tradition." The show includes satire based on life at Columbia University.

The production dates back to 1894 and has seen many famous performers and artists. Some of the most famous early Varsity Show members are Richard Rodgers and Oscar Hammerstein II, who composed and wrote many Broadway musicals under the name Rodgers and Hammerstein, including *The Sound of Music*, *Cinderella*, *Oklahoma!*, and *The King and I*. More recent notable Varsity Show alumni include Jenny Slate and Greta Gerwig.

McKinnon was part of three Varsity Shows: "Dial D for Deadline," "Off-Broadway," and "The Sound of Muses." It was in this space that she really honed her talent as a sketch comedian. McKinnon told Rachel Dunphy of the *Columbia Daily Spectator*, "I learned a lot about sketch comedy while doing the Varsity Show. Having to create characters and pitch them, having to do monologues and then improvise as them. It really is great training for sketch comedy."

While at Columbia, Kate also cofounded a comedy group called Tea Party. The group performed musical improv comedy. Improv comedy, short for "improvisation," is a kind of live theater in which the dialogue of a scene is made up on the spot. Improv actors need to be quick on their feet to come up with dialogue to keep the scene moving. McKinnon told Shuster of *Columbia College Today* of her time at the Varsity Show, "I didn't know it at the time, but I was learning the tools of sketch comedy and improv comedy." McKinnon used these tools in her time working on Tea Party. Tea Party performances also used McKinnon's musical talents, since much of the music came from her piano.

McKinnon's senior thesis was a one-woman show, titled *The Samantha Show*, which included both funny characters and a personal connection to her own life. McKinnon graduated from Columbia University's theater program in 2006, and her time at the Varsity Show continues to have a special place in her heart. She would never forget Columbia, just as Columbia would not forget her.

In 2013, Kate McKinnon won the I. A. L. Diamond Award for Achievement in the Arts from Columbia

University. The award goes to alumni of either Columbia University or its sister college, Barnard. The winner is someone "who has demonstrated continued commitment to, and has found success in, the arts." It is the highest honor given to a member of the Varsity Show.

When McKinnon accepted the award, she said that this was the one award that she wanted to receive in her life. "Honestly, I thought about it all the time. I didn't think I would, but I hoped I would," she told Dunphy of the *Columbia Daily Spectator*. About her time at Columbia and the Varsity show, McKinnon said, "To be able to continue to do comedy beyond this is a real dream come true, and the dream really began here."

CHAPTER TWO

A Sketchy Start

McKinnon may be best known for her work on *Saturday Night Live*, but she performed sketch comedy for many years before her breakout performances there. She is a master at writing characters who are both real and satirical and tickle the funny bone of her audience. Over the years, she looked for opportunities to create new characters and share them with the world.

A Life-Changing Audition

McKinnon's first big comedy opportunity came before she even graduated from Columbia University. She was chosen to be one of the first cast members of *The Big Gay Sketch Show*. The show was first aired on Logo, a television network started by MTV. Its main focus is creating quality television for LGBT viewers. Logo and *The Big Gay Sketch Show* were a step in a more progressive direction for television when the show premiered in 2007.

The Big Gay Sketch Show had both music-based and traditional sketches, performed by its eight cast members. The show featured recurring characters played by the cast. It also had pop culture parodies, or works that imitate something that already exists to poke fun at it. The show was a collaboration of many talented LGBT individuals, including Rosie O'Donnell. O'Donnell, a famous lesbian comedian and activist, was one of the executive producers of the show. The director was lesbian actress and comedian Amanda Bearse.

McKinnon, a senior at Columbia during the casting for the show, wanted in. She heard about the audition from her best friend. When McKinnon showed up at the open call, there were around three hundred people trying out for a spot on the new show. It took six weeks for Logo to choose their cast, a time during which McKinnon admits she was nervous. She told Shuster of *Columbia College Today* how she was unable to look for a job or even do her schoolwork while she was waiting to hear back. She said, "Comedy is important to me and to have a show that is just about how funny it is to be gay seems like a good thing. I was desperate to be involved in that."

Luckily, McKinnon nailed her last audition, performing a few hilarious characters. She got the job before graduating—a dream come true.

In college, McKinnon dreamed of finding work as an actress. Today, her career has skyrocketed, thanks to her success on *Saturday Night Live* and movies like *Ghostbusters*.

McKinnon told Shuster of *Columbia College Today*, "It's like I had gotten a shortcut to where I wanted to be, instead of toiling for years and possibly quitting before I had a chance to do anything."

A Calling and a Miracle

McKinnon brought many characters to *The Big Gay Sketch Show*. McKinnon says that her favorite character to perform was Fitzwilliam, a British boy who longs to be a girl. Playing a male role is not a problem for McKinnon, who often plays both male and female characters, even in her work today on *SNL*. She said that her time filming the first season of *The Big Gay Sketch Show* was the best few weeks of her whole life.

For McKinnon, there was a bigger reason behind being on the show. It was not just a job for her—it was a calling. She told Logo in an interview, "I've been an out and proud lesbian since I was twelve years old so it's highly exciting to me that there is a gay sketch show and that I get to be on it is just, like, a miracle. It's not just some sketch show. I feel like I'm doing it for my people."

McKinnon performed in all three seasons of *The Big Gay Sketch Show*. It was around this time that she decided to go by her first and middle name—Kate McKinnon—and starting to gain a name for herself in the national LGBT and sketch comedy communities.

Even though McKinnon caught a big break with *The Big Gay Sketch Show*, she admits that there were many years of struggle before she made much money from her comedy. After she graduated, she had no real full-time job or source of income. Living in one of the most expensive cities in the world—New York—McKinnon had to find ways to make enough money to survive, usually by odd jobs.

Right after college, McKinnon worked in telemarketing, which meant that she tried to sell things over the phone. There were days McKinnon was not sure she would be able to find work in comedy. McKinnon admitted to Mehera Bonner of *Marie Claire* that if she were not in comedy, she would probably live in the woods and be a carpenter. Luckily for her fans, this never happened. However, even after she was cast in *SNL,* she claimed that her plan in five years was to just be employed still. She said, "To be employed in the entertainment industry is a miracle. Every day I look in the mirror and think 'Holy crap, I'm employed.'"

Working for Laughs

Even though she did not have a regularly paying job in comedy right away, McKinnon found ways to keep busy and find her audience. In 2008, she brought her

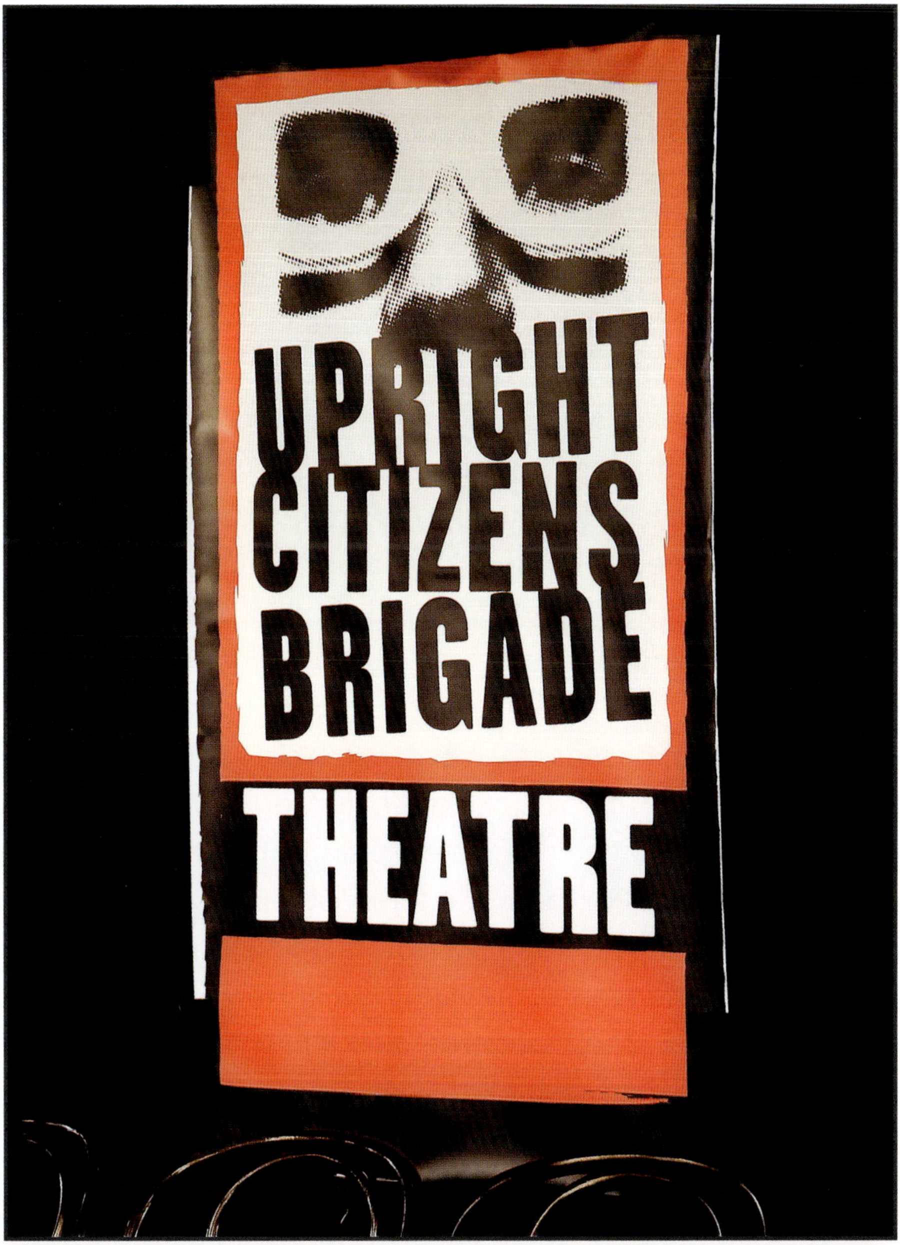

The famous and funny Upright Citizen's Brigade has four locations—two in New York City and two in Los Angeles, California. Fans of comedy can catch a show at any of these theaters.

talents to the Upright Citizens Brigade. The Upright Citizens Brigade is one of the best-known improv groups in the country. They have an improv training center as well. Today, it is still possible to catch a show at the Upright Citizens Brigade Theater seven days a week at their multiple theater locations. Upright Citizens Brigade members perform sketch shows, improv, stand-up comedy, and more, and it is one of the most respected improv schools in the country. Interestingly, the group does not pay its comedians. However, participants gain a wealth of skills, knowledge, and connections in the entertainment business.

Before the Upright Citizens Brigade was founded, there was not much in the way of improv in New York City. The opportunities for improv actors and comedians were mostly in Chicago, Illinois, thanks to the world famous comedy troupe Second City. A few improv actors decided to leave Chicago and start something new in New York City in 1996. The founders—also known as the UCB Four—included Matt Besser, Matt Walsh, Ian Roberts, and Amy Poehler. These comedians brought all they had learned in Chicago to New York City, and, in doing so, shaped the careers of many famous actors and comedians. Famous members of the Upright Citizens Brigade include

MORE POEHLER, PLEASE

Amy Poehler and Kate McKinnon have a lot in common. They both got their start with improv and sketch comedy on stage before landing starring roles on *SNL*. They are both voice actors and film actors. Poehler was one of the founders of the Upright Citizens Brigade, which McKinnon later joined. They have both played the important role of Hillary Clinton on *SNL*.

Poehler is one of the most successful female comedic actresses in the United States. Getting her start with Second City improv troupe in Chicago, she moved to New York City to start the Upright Citizens Brigade in 1996. In 2001, Poehler was cast on *SNL*, where she was known for her impressions of celebrities

Amy Poehler is one of the queens of twenty-first century comedy. After starting small in Chicago, she has gone on to become a major television and movie star.

(continued on the next page)

(continued from the previous page)

and politicians, from Hillary Clinton to Kelly Ripa, and for her role on the recurring *SNL* news segment Weekend Update. She starred in the hit show *Parks and Recreation,* and has acted in several hit comedic films such as *Blades of Glory, Mean Girls,* and *Baby Mama.*

Sasheer Zamata, Ed Helms, Aziz Ansari, and Aubrey Plaza.

McKinnon was a natural fit for the Upright Citizens Brigade. Willing to work hard even for no money, McKinnon gained exposure and attention for her performances there. She joined several sketch comedy teams within the Upright Citizens Brigade, including High Treason, Beneath Gristedes, Tremendous Machine, and Gramps. While performing and filming these sketch shows, she was able to work with comedians who would later become her costars at *SNL*, including Bobby Moynihan and Sasheer Zamata.

McKinnon tried her hand at all kinds of comedy performances. She performed stand-up comedy, delivering jokes onstage to an audience. She also

UCB has produced a long list of successful comedians, including Bobby Moynihan, who has worked with Kate McKinnon on *SNL* and as a voice actor on the PBS show *Nature Cat*.

performed a number of one-woman shows with the Upright Citizens Brigade. McKinnon's solo shows included *Disenchanted*, *Best Actress*, and *Kate McKinnon on Ice*.

One-person shows in comedy are also called solo sketch comedy. This is very different from stand-up comedy, a show in which the comedian directly addresses the audience. In solo sketch comedy, the comedian acts as one or even multiple characters, typically performing a full-length show all by themselves. Solo shows give comics a chance to explore the range of acting they are able to do, and they are an opportunity for a comedic writer and performer to get many of his or her characters onto the stage and into the headlines.

In these years between college and *SNL*, McKinnon may not have been making much money, but she was mastering her craft. She was surrounded by some of the best improv and sketch actors and writers in the country. She was writing new sketches and coming up with new characters. This important time in McKinnon's life is when she started to find her voice—or voices. Fortunately for McKinnon, her work did not go unnoticed.

She was about to get her big break.

CHAPTER THREE

Saturday Night Live Superstar

For any sketch comedy performer in the United States, the dream is to be cast on *Saturday Night Live*. Regular viewers tune in to NBC every Saturday night to see what the cast has cooked up. For many, it is a tradition to watch the show, keeping up with comedians who start out as relatively unknown and end up famous, such as Bill Murray and Tina Fey. During a normal year, the show might draw seven million viewers. During election years, when the cast weighs in on political events, that number can climb to nearly nine million viewers. It is an American tradition.

McKinnon recounted how her father encouraged her to watch *SNL* growing up. Along with Mel Brooks movies, the show was one of her greatest teachers as a kid. Perhaps it comes as no surprise that after years of sketch comedy at *The Big Gay Sketch Show* and the Upright Citizens Brigade, McKinnon decided to try out for her own chance at the dream in 2012.

The Chance of a Lifetime

McKinnon told Liam Berry and Mary Green of *People* magazine about her initial *SNL* interview, recalling, "It was very scary. If you're a sketch comedian, *SNL* is the job you want to get … It's so important in the history of American culture, and it was such an important part of my life growing up." McKinnon recalled how nervous she was to impress Lorne Michaels—a huge name in American show business—in such a short period of time.

Lorne Michaels is the director of *SNL*, and he is known for finding great talent in comedy and showcasing it to the world. He is also known to be quite tough on comedians. McKinnon told Berry and Green of *People*, "The first time you walk in the building, it's like you're seeing the Wizard of Oz. Except he's not fake, he's real, he's sitting at a table, and you're doing comedy for him." She recalled it as a defining moment in her own life. During the audition, McKinnon presented her best celebrity impressions and a few good characters, hoping it would be enough to win over Michaels.

McKinnon stands with the cast of *SNL* at the 2017 Emmy Awards ceremony. McKinnon won an Emmy for Outstanding Supporting Actress, and *SNL* won an Emmy for Outstanding Variety Sketch Series.

Michaels was not the only one in the room. When a comedian auditions for *SNL*, cast members can sit in on the audition. However, they are not allowed to laugh. Famous comedian and former *SNL* actor Bill Hader remembers McKinnon's audition. He also remembers being removed from the room. In 2018, he told Ellen DeGeneres on her talk show, "When Kate McKinnon came on, she started her audition and I started laughing so hard that they were like, 'Get Bill out of here.' I thought she was unreal."

McKinnon won over both Lorne Michaels and the cast members. She got the job. In April 2012, McKinnon started work on *Saturday Night Live*, filling the spot vacated by Kristen Wiig. Wiig, who was nominated for several Emmys for *SNL*, had left McKinnon some big shoes to fill.

THE WIIG PARTY

Kristen Wiig is perhaps best known for her starring role in the 2011 award-winning movie *Bridesmaids.* The movie reshaped the way people saw women in comedy with its largely female cast, proving that women could be hard-hitters in the an industry historically dominated by men.

Wiig started her improv and sketch career with the Groundlings, a comedy troupe based in Los Angeles, California. In 2005, she was hired on *SNL,* where she was known for her funny characters and impressions, which included Speaker of the House Nancy Pelosi, television show host Elisabeth Hasselbeck, and television show host Kathie Lee Gifford.

Kristen Wiig left *SNL* in 2012, just as McKinnon was starting. However, the two worked together on the movie *Ghostbusters: Answer the Call* in 2016.

Kristen Wiig is shown here posing for a picture at the Los Angeles premiere of *Ghostbusters: Answer the Call* in 2016.

That same year, Wiig came back to host *SNL*. Wiig played a guest role on McKinnon's recurring sketch "Whiskers R We," where McKinnon plays the character Barbara DeDrew.

Crazy Characters and Impressive Impressions

McKinnon got to work proving herself as a cast member right away, joining in on sketches and writing some of her own characters. Some of McKinnon's best-known characters are Barbara DeDrew, Olya Povlatsky, and Mrs. Rafferty.

Barbara DeDrew is a character who runs "Whiskers R We," trying to get people to adopt cats. The character is known for her cat puns, and many celebrities have joined in this recurring sketch, including Melissa McCarthy, Kristen Wiig, and Amy Adams. Olya Povlatsky is a character who often joins *SNL*'s news segment, Weekend Update, to weigh in on current events through the lens of her upbringing in Russia. Her character points to the poverty of rural Russia in a straightforward way, which is both funny and sad. Mrs. Rafferty is a woman who keeps getting abducted by aliens and has a much worse experience than any of her friends during the abduction.

McKinnon is also known for her impressions, which cover celebrities and politicians alike. One of her most famous celebrity impressions is Justin Bieber. She is able to capture what she sees as the boyishness in Bieber, his charm, and his unique voice and movements. She wears full-arm temporary tattoos and his signature

Justin Bieber became an international singing sensation at the age of thirteen. McKinnon's impression of Bieber shows both his youth and the "bad boy" image he tries to show to the world.

blonde hair. Bieber often tries to be a "bad boy," something that McKinnon pokes fun at. McKinnon is very comfortable doing both male and female impressions, and nothing seems too far of a stretch. Bieber was one of the first men McKinnon had to impersonate on the show. She told Hunt and O'Connell of *Hollywood Reporter,* "I was thrilled because I hadn't gotten to play boys before and now I've made kind of a habit of it. I am very grateful that they let me do that."

McKinnon also does an impression of a woman she admires greatly: Ellen DeGeneres. McKinnon wears Ellen's signature short hair, pants, and sweater sets and incorporates many of Ellen's sayings and behaviors. After playing DeGeneres on *SNL*, McKinnon was invited onto *The Ellen DeGeneres Show* in 2013. DeGeneres surprised McKinnon with an outfit to match her own and had McKinnon impersonate her right on the spot. Afterward, they danced up and down the aisles.

When McKinnon came back on the show in 2016, DeGeneres said, "It's weird to have somebody do impressions of you because when you hear it, you're like, well that's such an exaggeration, I mean it's funny, but it doesn't sound like me at all. The next day your friends call you up and say, 'Did you see Kate on *SNL*? She sounded exactly like you.'"

BRINGING RBG TO LIFE

Ruth Bader Ginsburg has been a Supreme Court Justice since 1993. She has been a voice for justice for decades, known to dissent—or hold a different opinion from—the other justices. She never set out to be a celebrity. However, with the help of Kate McKinnon's impersonation of her on *SNL*, Ginsburg became a cultural icon. Now, Ginsburg is the subject of a movie about her life, a role model for many young people, and she is affectionately known to some as RBG. McKinnon turned a political figure into a superhero for many viewers of *SNL*.

McKinnon often plays Ginsburg on the news segment Weekend Update. She portrays Ginsburg as a very tiny, old woman who can still pack a punch, with one-line zingers and a spunky personality. The character

(continued on the next page)

Justice Ruth Bader Ginsburg may be the oldest justice on the Supreme Court, but she does not let that slow her down. She is still an active voice for justice, and McKinnon enjoys portraying her.

(continued from the previous page)

often says how she is never going to leave the Supreme Court, even though she is in her eighties. McKinnon coined the phrase "Ginsburn" for when Justice Ginsburg delivers an insult to her opponent. Ginsburg loves McKinnon's impression of her, telling Joyce Chen of *Rolling Stone,* "I liked the actress who portrayed me [McKinnon] and I would like to say 'Gins-Burn' sometimes to my colleagues."

Part of pulling off a funny impression is making the audience believe—even partially—that they are seeing the genuine article. It is clear that McKinnon not only enjoys acting like DeGeneres, she is also very skilled at it.

McKinnon does make fun of her subjects and exaggerate their behaviors, but she also tries to understand them as people. She told Amy Wallace of *GQ,* "You can't be judging someone as you're embodying them. You have to find the point of connection—something you find delightful." McKinnon has played characters that she does not agree with politically, including Kellyanne Conway, an advisor to President Donald Trump. Even so, she is able to dig deep and find some kind of empathy for the person. She said, "Even if you're intending to skewer someone, you also have to find something that you truly like about them. If you're mean, it ain't fun to watch. And if it ain't fun to watch, they turn off the TV."

A Comedian and a Writer

In her interview with Hunt and O'Connell of *Hollywood Reporter* in 2016, McKinnon was asked how much of an impact she has on the impersonations she does on *SNL.* She responded, "We have a huge impact on it because we participate in the writing of it." As a cast member at *SNL*, McKinnon has to act and write, as well as take direction from the other writers and cast members. It is truly a team effort, and she is often taking the lead.

Writing normally happens on Tuesdays. McKinnon retreats to her office and writes in silence, in between chatting with her costars and pitching ideas. Saturday night skits are often based on the current events of the week, so writers and cast members have to be on alert for current political or celebrity events. These events are often included in the cold open, or the opening skit of the show. The show is a living thing throughout the week that can change at any time.

On Saturdays, there is a rush to get everything together before the show goes live. McKinnon compares Saturdays at *SNL* to a sporting event.

She told Wallace of *GQ* that Saturdays require both physical and mental focus. She said, "There is, quite literally, a clock ticking down throughout the day. It's scary. And thrilling. You know: Are we going to win, or not?"

Around *SNL*, McKinnon is respected as a comedy genius, both as a performer and a writer. Former writer Chris Kelly told Wallace of *GQ*, "Kate is always, always, always fighting to make something better. Make a joke funnier. Make a sketch sharper." Kelly recalled how McKinnon is in a constant state of creativity, always writing, even when the show is about to start. He said, "She'll run up to you in the hall with a crumpled-up little script, just covered in pitches."

When asked by Hunt and O'Connell of *Hollywood Reporter* where she thinks comedy comes from, she said, "For me, I start from a place of exploiting things in me that I find objectionable and displaying them and celebrating them." From her work on the sketch comedy stages of Columbia University to the big-time at *Saturday Night Live*, McKinnon has celebrated the objectionable to great success, winning two Emmys for her work on the late-night show and gaining fans around the world.

CHAPTER FOUR

The Comedy of Politics

What does comedy have to do with politics? How can anyone find anything funny about what goes on in the government? Can comedy have an effect on the politics of a nation?

They may seem unrelated, but politics have a noticeable effect on comedy, and shows like *Saturday Night Live* do impact the discussion of politics in the United States and around the world. Satire has long been used to talk about what is going on politically. It is a voice for the common person who looks at absurd political issues and feels they have no power but to laugh at them. Satire helps turn a political situation on its head and look at it from a different light—often to great effect.

Poking at Politics

From its very first show, *SNL* has weighed in on politics, poking fun at both Republican and Democratic politicians. While *SNL* claims to be nonpartisan—meaning not directly in support of any political party—it often seems to lean liberal. However, the show is not afraid to jab at the strange behaviors and shortcomings of anyone in the public eye.

Chevy Chase (*right*) is shown here impersonating President Gerald Ford in the Oval Office in this *Saturday Night Live* sketch from 1976. Some believe Chase's Ford impression had a negative effect on his re-election campaign.

In 1976, when the show was still new, comedian and actor Chevy Chase acted as then-president Gerald Ford, portraying Ford as incompetent and unintelligent. Ford even claimed that *SNL* was the reason he did not win his reelection bid that year. That was not the last impact the show would have on a presidential election. The show is heavily viewed in election years and makes a huge difference in how viewers perceive candidates. In 2000, *SNL*'s portrayal of Al Gore, a Democratic presidential candidate, may have been the reason fewer people voted for him than expected.

In 2008, Tina Fey played Sarah Palin, who hoped to be vice president on John McCain's Republican ticket. Fey's portrayal of Palin was so similar in look, speech, and behavior that people started seeing the impersonation when they thought of Palin. Fey, acting as Palin, famously joked that she could see Russia from her backyard. Because of how authentic Fey's impression was, many people believed that Palin, proudly from Alaska, actually said these words, but she certainly did not. Though this impression was not the only reason McCain lost the 2008 election, it was undeniably a factor.

McKinnon Makes Her Mark

Kate McKinnon was already a star on *SNL* before the 2016 election started heating up. However, it

McKinnon, who plays Hillary Clinton, is shown here with Alec Baldwin, who plays Donald Trump on *SNL*. Though the two are often fighting during their impressions, Baldwin and McKinnon get along very well.

was her role in the portrayal of the election that cemented her as a household name. McKinnon was cast in the important role of Hillary Clinton, who competed against Bernie Sanders (played by comedian Larry David) in the Democratic primaries, and then against Republican candidate Donald Trump (played by Alec Baldwin) in the presidential election. If Clinton won, America would see its first female president, and McKinnon was hoping that would be the outcome.

McKinnon told *Vanity Fair*'s Lili Anolik that she loves playing politicians because she gets to imagine the private lives of people who try so hard to project a polished public image. She gets to the heart and humanity of those people. She said, "In doing that for Hillary Clinton, who I admire so much, I started to feel very close to her, just trying to imagine her inner life."

McKinnon was very excited about the opportunity to possibly play the first female president of the United States. In her portrayal of Clinton, McKinnon told *Hollywood Reporter*'s Hunt and O'Connell that she saw a contrast between a woman who was driven in her goals and hardened by her experiences. McKinnon saw a woman who wanted to win the election, but also saw that the country needed her to win the election. She also saw a "little sweetie granny from the Midwest." McKinnon hoped to bring all of these characteristics to the national spotlight. When McKinnon thought about meeting Clinton, she said she would be nervous to meet her because she finds her so "resplendent."

McKinnon's portrayal of Hillary Clinton showed a woman who was trying hard to connect to people, because of how much she really wanted to lead them. The election was Clinton's chance to make a difference, and McKinnon played a character desperate to show her smarts, her skills, and her passion. McKinnon's Clinton was often unable to comprehend how her competition even came close to matching her experience and talents. McKinnon also took little loving jabs at the fact that Clinton had to really make a conscious to act like a "cool" candidate, when really, she was more focused on the political issues—not on how she was perceived by others.

On the season premiere of *SNL* in 2015, Clinton appeared alongside McKinnon on the show. The sketch started with McKinnon, as Clinton, at the bar, complaining about the fact that people are drawn to Republican candidates. She says, "Why won't the people just let me lead? Just give me the hammer and the nails and let me fix it all." Then, McKinnon calls over the bartender, Val, who is played by Hillary Clinton. The chemistry between the two is clear as they talk about political issues. McKinnon barbs Clinton in the sketch, talking about how it took a while for her to support gay rights. Clinton, as Val, took all the jokes in stride, saying, "Fair point." The two end the sketch with their arms around each other's shoulders, singing the song "Lean on Me." The sketch humanized Clinton as a candidate and gave McKinnon a big chance to meet her hero.

On November 8, 2016, the presidential race came to a close. Hillary Clinton had lost, and Donald Trump had won. While Clinton had won the popular vote by a significant margin, Trump had won in the electoral college. For many Democrats, this was a hard loss to take. For McKinnon—who had embodied Hillary Clinton for months and looked up to her—it was devastating. Many *SNL* viewers tuned in that Saturday to make sense of all that had

Hillary Clinton is shown here speaking during a presidential debate in 2016. During the election season, McKinnon embodied Clinton's smarts, eagerness to lead, and her annoyance at her opponent, Donald Trump.

happened, not knowing how the show would deal with something so shocking and, to some, heartbreaking.

The cold open was simple that night—Kate McKinnon playing "Hallelujah" on the piano while dressed as Hillary Clinton, belting the words, "And even though it all went wrong, I'll stand before the lord of song with nothing on my tongue but hallelujah." McKinnon's genuine emotion over the loss was obvious during the performance, which is one of the most iconic moments in recent *SNL* history.

Not Giving Up

Just as she said in her "Hallelujah" performance, McKinnon was not ready to give up after the election. She was ready to take on new personas and shape the political landscape yet again with new impersonations.

The Donald Trump presidency introduced America to a new cast of political players and therefore a new cast of characters for *SNL*'s actors and actresses. While Alec Baldwin played Trump and Melissa McCarthy played White House press secretary Sean Spicer in a gender-bending role, McKinnon truly stole the show with her wide array of political impersonations.

COMEDIAN AND POLITICIAN: A SISTERHOOD

Did Hillary Clinton appreciate McKinnon's impersonations? After the election, Clinton did an interview with Jimmy Fallon on *The Tonight Show Starring Jimmy Fallon*. She said McKinnon's "Hallelujah" performance was a "tearjerker." She told Fallon that watching McKinnon play that song way really hard for her. She said McKinnon was "actually a better me than I am, to be honest." She also praised the actress, saying, "I wish I had her talent. She's just an amazing person."

On McKinnon's side, she was so grateful to play Clinton that she mentioned her in her Emmy speech in 2017. McKinnon, who normally does not show emotion out of character, cried as she said, "Being part of this season of *Saturday Night Live* was the most meaningful thing I will ever do … On a very personal note, I want to say thank you to Hillary Clinton for your grace and grit." On the *Today* show in 2016, McKinnon said she felt a sense of sisterhood with Clinton after meeting her. While many people have played Clinton through the years—including the famous Amy Poehler—it seems McKinnon embodied her true spirit.

One of McKinnon's harshest impressions was of Kellyanne Conway. Conway worked as the campaign manager of Trump's campaign before being named counselor to the president when Trump was elected. In one sketch after the inauguration, McKinnon played Conway during a press interview, evading questions about Russian interference in the election by changing the subject. McKinnon plays Conway as power-hungry, fame-hungry, and not afraid to lie to save face. In one particularly scathing sketch, McKinnon plays Conway as if she were Pennywise the clown from Stephen King's horror novel *It*. In the sketch, Kellyanne lurks in a sewer, waiting for CNN's Anderson Cooper to walk by, and tries to get him to let her back on television, desperate for attention.

McKinnon also played a few male political players, including Jeff Sessions and Robert Mueller. These roles once again showed that McKinnon was comfortable with playing both male and female roles and also roles on both sides of the political aisle. She has already established herself as one of the most versatile members of the *SNL* cast.

When Jeff Sessions became attorney general of the United States, much of the country was in an uproar. Loyal *SNL* viewers wondered who would play him in the inevitable sketches on the show. It was a surprise when McKinnon showed up in a

Many Americans disliked the appointment of Jeff Sessions to the position of attorney general. McKinnon has poked fun at the politician's slow speech and old-fashioned ideas in her *SNL* impressions.

Forrest Gump-themed sketch, in a suit with slicked-back white hair. She played on Sessions's Southern accent and singlemindedness. In sketches after this, she often played Sessions with a tail and rodent-like features, making it seem as if Sessions were a rat.

In 2017, the United States Department of Justice launched a special investigation into the 2016 presidential election. Many believe that Russia meddled in the election and that Trump's campaign took part in it. Special counsel Robert Mueller was put in charge of the investigation—and McKinnon was put in charge of playing Mueller on *SNL.* McKinnon plays the normally stone-faced Mueller as charming, confident, and cool under pressure. McKinnon's Mueller knows he has some juicy lead in the investigation, but will not tell anyone what it is. McKinnon plays Mueller like a sort of superhero, the answer to many people's call for justice.

Who will McKinnon play next? With an ever-shifting cast of politicians, *SNL* will never run out of characters to play. McKinnon's ability to find the inner spirit of her characters, to play up their ridiculous features while also humanizing them, makes her an obvious choice for a wide range of celebrities and politicians.

CHAPTER FIVE

McKinnon Goes to Hollywood

By 2016, Kate McKinnon's career was taking off. She was one of the most popular comedians in the United States, thanks to her Hillary Clinton impression. That year, she would make her way from the small screen to the silver screen. She proved to everyone that she was a versatile actress—able to take on characters in sketch comedy and bring characters alive from a movie script. She also has talent as both a voice actor in cartoons and a major part of a blockbuster film.

An All-Girl *Ghostbusters*

Kate McKinnon's big break in Hollywood came with the premiere of *Ghostbusters: Answer the Call* in 2016. The movie was a reboot of the movie *Ghostbusters*, which originally came out in 1984.

This promotional image for *Ghostbusters: Answer the Call* shows McKinnon in costume as Dr. Jillian Holtzmann. Her performance as Holtzmann was widely praised.

The 1984 *Ghostbusters* told the story of four men who start a ghost removal business. Along the way, they have to fight many kinds of supernatural beings, using their knowledge of the paranormal and their ghost-busting proton packs. The movie became a cult classic, or a film with a large following. It starred Dan Aykroyd, Harold Ramis, Rick Moranis, and Bill Murray. Dan Aykroyd and Bill Murray also got their start as comedians on *SNL.*

This still from the original *Ghostbusters* movie shows the all-star cast— (*left to right*) Harold Ramis, Dan Akroyd, Ernie Hudson, and Bill Murray.

Aykroyd was part of the original cast of *SNL* from 1975 to 1979, while Murray acted on the show from 1977 to 1980. *Ghostbusters* became one of the highest-earning movies of the 1980s, and it seemed everyone knew the theme song, which asked the question, "Who you gonna call? Ghostbusters!"

The new reboot of *Ghostbusters* had big comedy shoes to fill. It had to take a fresh spin on the classic movie. Director Paul Feig turned the movie on its head with an all-female cast. For years, there had been a debate in the comedy world: Are women funny enough to star in a major comedy film? Feig proved that not only are women funny, but they can breathe new life into an old classic.

Feig says he actually did not set out to make such a huge statement casting four women as the Ghostbusters. He told Jada Yua of *Vulture*, "There wasn't even a thought about gender. It was just, 'These guys are all funny. We're going to do it.' I never thought it was male-exclusive. None of us did." However, he soon found that a lot people hated the idea, which he chalked up to misogyny, or men thinking they are better than women. There was even a campaign to make the 2016 *Ghostbusters* trailer the most disliked in YouTube history. Even with the controversy surrounding the film, Feig delivered a successful movie with a star-studded cast. The movie won Favorite Movie at the Kids' Choice Awards and a Saturn Award for Best Fantasy Film from the Academy of Science Fiction, Fantasy, & Horror. McKinnon herself won praise for her performance, which launched her from sketch comedian to Hollywood star.

McKinnon's character is Dr. Jillian Holtzmann. She is a hardware expert and genius scientist who has the ability to build new and improved equipment for getting rid of ghosts. She wears signature yellow-tinted goggles, has wild hair, and dons a quirky wardrobe of leather jackets and overalls. Angela Watercutter of *Wired* said of the character, “She’s part mad scientist, part super freak, and all heart.” Manohla Dargis of the *New York Times* said, “Ms. McKinnon makes for a sublime nerd goddess ... Here, she embodies the new ‘Ghostbusters’ at its best: Girls rule, women are funny, get over it.”

Director Feig actually wrote the part of Dr. Jillian Holtzmann around Kate McKinnon’s talents and personality. He did an interview with McKinnon, in character, and asked her questions about Holtzmann’s backstory. Her humor is clear throughout many of Holtzmann’s funniest moments. McKinnon delivers many of the movie’s memorable lines, such as when she calls the Pringles she is eating “salty parabolas.” Additionally, her character is hypothesized to be a lesbian, so many in the LGBT community eagerly accepted her as a hero.

McKinnon won praise for her acting in the movie. She brought her own style to the character, and many people say that her signature humor carried the movie. Ann Hornaday of the *Washington Post* wrote, “McKinnon’s Holtzmann is the straw that stirs the drink throughout ‘Ghostbusters,’ her performance one that easily could have been an exercise in phoned-in snark, but instead proves to be an example of genuinely smart, specific and confoundingly funny characterization."

McKinnon won the Women's Film Critics Circle Award for Best Comedic Actress for her role in *Ghostbusters.* She was also a nominee for a Critics Choice Award for Best Actress in a Comedy, a Kids' Choice Award, and a Saturn Award. Though not every critic agreed on the quality of the movie itself, it seems all critics loved McKinnon's part in it. One thing was clear—Dr. Jillian Holtzmann was not only a perfect fit for McKinnon, it was her breakout Hollywood role.

Small Parts, Big Laughs

After *Ghostbusters*, McKinnon landed some smaller roles in movies. In 2016, she acted in the holiday movie *Office Christmas Party*. Her character, Mary, works in human resources and takes office rules very seriously. She wears a multi-denominational holiday sweater with Christmas, Hanukkah, Kwanza, and other holiday symbols on it. She is uptight, yet quirky, and McKinnon brought her own silly style to the character.

In 2017, McKinnon acted in the movie *Rough Night*, starring Scarlett Johansson. The movie is about a bachelorette weekend gone wrong. McKinnon plays the main character's friend from

THE MANY VOICES OF KATE MCKINNON

Kate McKinnon is the queen of impressions, changing her voice to suit whoever she is impersonating. This skill makes her the perfect fit for voice acting. In 2016 alone, McKinnon lent her voice to three major movies: *Finding Dory, Leap!,* and *The Angry Birds Movie.*

In 2017, she voiced the character of Lupe in *Ferdinand,* an animated film by Bly Sky Studios about a large bull who would rather smell flowers than participate in bull fights. Lupe is a feisty, excitable goat that wants to be Ferdinand's coach. The movie won a Golden Globe Award, and was nominated for an Oscar for Best Animated Feature Film. McKinnon told Gwynne Watkins of Yahoo!, "I just immediately connected with the idea of a goat with big dreams."

college, named Pippa. Pippa is from Australia, and so McKinnon embodied the character with a free-spirit energy and a strong Australian accent. Scott Tobias of *NPR* said, "It seems highly unlikely the part was written for an Australian, but her instincts—and the instincts of her co-writer/director, Lucia

Aniello—prevailed and the film is funnier because of it."

With these successful roles behind her—in addition to her ever expanding stable of characters on *SNL*—McKinnon is making quite a name for herself in the world of comedy. Her versatility has allowed her to play roles that many other comedians would not be able to pull off, and that is a talent impossible to teach.

An International Spy Sensation

In 2018, Kate McKinnon got the chance to be a costar in a major movie: *The Spy Who Dumped Me*. Her costar was Mila Kunis, who has been a big name in movies and television for a long time. The movie is about two best friends, Audrey (Kunis) and Morgan (McKinnon) who find themselves in the middle of an international scheme, with assassins on their trail. They travel throughout Europe on a mission to stay alive and save the world.

The movie came out to mixed reviews, with many people surprised by how many characters were killed in the movie. There were many stunts and a lot of bodies. A. O. Scott of the *New York Times* called it a "pleasantly silly, sometimes jarringly violent comedy." Many viewed the film as a buddy comedy, which is a genre that gets its

This still from *The Spy Who Dumped Me* shows Kate McKinnon and Mila Kunis as best friends Morgan and Audrey.

comedic value from the banter and interactions between the two main characters. Others, however, saw it as a run-of-the-mill action movie. The disconnect between these two genres led some critics to respond negatively to the film.

Despite mixed reviews, McKinnon won mostly praise for her role as Morgan, an aspiring actor and fierce feminist. Owen Gleiberman of *Variety* wrote, "at least one dimension of 'The Spy Who Dumped Me' is fully alive, and that's Kate McKinnon's twinkle-of-killer-attitude performance. There are moments she salvages the movie."

The movie was filmed throughout Europe, including the Netherlands, Germany, Austria, Denmark, Czech Republic, and Hungary. McKinnon made the most of her time traveling. She recounted to late-night talk show host Jimmy Fallon that she tried to learn Hungarian by studying every day for three months. However, because it is such a difficult language, she could not even order off a menu confidently. Instead, she had her Hungarian driver teach her how to rap in the language. McKinnon rapped the song on *The Tonight Show with Jimmy Fallon*, with perfect Hungarian pronunciation and her trademark confidence and quirk.

McKinnon has proved in her young acting career that she is ready to take on any quirky character in comedy, even in major films. Many critics think her comedy carries the movie she is a part of. From Hungarian rapping to action scenes, McKinnon is a true jack-of-all-trades.

CHAPTER SIX

Gay in the Spotlight

Not everyone in the spotlight chooses to discuss their sexual orientation—especially those who are gay, lesbian, bisexual, or queer. In the past, being "found out" to be gay could ruin a career. For that reason, many people in show business have chosen to stay closeted instead of tell the world who they really are. Some people, such as Ellen DeGeneres, have chosen to "come out" after many years of building a career. Some people, including the first lesbian member of *Saturday Night Live*—Danitra Vance—choose to keep their personal life hidden.

Kate McKinnon, though an introvert, is not one to keep things hidden. As she told Rebecca Keegan of the *LA Times*, "I tried for a short time to be something I wasn't, and had no success with it. It's a practical solution to just be yourself."

BREAKING (SOME) BARRIERS

Danitra Vance was born in Chicago in 1954. She studied theater at the Webber-Douglas Academy of Dramatic Art in London, England. Like many comedians at the time, she got her start at Second City, a sketch comedy group in Chicago. She then moved to New York City, where she created a cast of characters for her 1981 off-Broadway show titled *Danitra Vance and the Mell-o White Boys*.

In 1985, Vance became the first black woman to join the *SNL* cast. She was also the first member of the cast to have a known learning disability. Her dyslexia often made it difficult for her to memorize her lines and read from cue cards. Unknown to the public, she was also the first lesbian member of the

As its first lesbian cast member, Danitra Vance was a trailblazing member of the *Saturday Night Live* cast. Hired in 1985, Vance stayed on the show for one season.

cast. She decided to keep this a secret, until it was revealed after her early death at the age of forty. In her obituary, her partner—a woman named Jones Miller—was named at her request.

Growing Up Gay

Kate wondered what it meant to be gay when she was a child. Her mother explained that gay people like someone of the same sex and also tend to be creative. As a result, Kate did not grow up thinking this was a bad thing. When she hit her teens—and fell for Gillian Anderson, an actress on *The X-Files*—she knew it to be true about herself.

Being a private person, McKinnon finds it hard to talk about her personal life, except through character. She told Shuster of *Columbia College Today* that for most of high school, she tried very hard not to have feelings for people openly. She recalled the painful experience of falling in love with straight girls who she knew would not love her back.

McKinnon went to a small high school in Long Island with only a few hundred people. Coming out would have been a big deal and would have likely led to her being shut out by her peers. She even worried about her teachers treating her differently. She knew she would be physically safe, but she was afraid of being ridiculed. She worried people would make fun of her little sister, who also went to school there. She had to listen to people using "gay" as an insult. All that time, she held in her secret.

When Kate was fifteen, around the time her father became ill, she told her parents. Her mother's reaction was everything one would hope for. She was supportive and progressive in her beliefs about sexuality. Kate's father, however, became very religious the sicker he got. The Methodist Church he was a part of even helped raise funds for his medical bills. This strong religious belief—often a cause of friction with the gay community—could have come between him and Kate. However, Kate said that her father continued to be there for her and support her career in comedy.

Three years later, when she was eighteen, McKinnon came out to her little sister, Emily. She says that since then, Emily has become an advocate for LGBT causes, even though she is not gay herself.

After Ellen, a website devoted to lesbian and bisexual women in media, reported that McKinnon came out in high school in very theatrical ways—to both her theater camp and her Methodist church. She did both of these things on stage, a place where she feels comfortable. She would rather tell a crowd of a hundred people something than tell just one person. She has often recounted how it is actually more comfortable for her to perform in front of people she does not know than to have a straightforward conversation.

Out in Public

When McKinnon made it onto the cast of *The Big Gay Sketch Show*, there was no doubt about her sexuality. She was publicly out as a lesbian woman, and she decided to use that perspective in her comedy. After Ellen quoted McKinnon as saying, "As minorities, we're on the fringe, and there's just something so wonderful about that perspective, something so inspiring. If you're part of that minority, you can make fun of those people while respecting them and lifting them up."

McKinnon is aware that her ability to be out as a lesbian is in part because of the lesbian comedians who have come before her. It used to be a gamble to come out in comedy. One of the most famous lesbian comedians in the world is Ellen DeGeneres. Today, she has one of the most successful talk shows in America and is known for her generous and giving nature and her funny interviews with celebrities. However, when she came out in 1997, Ellen lost a lot of what she had worked for, including sponsors for her hit show *Ellen*, and then the show itself. Today, McKinnon has a close relationship with DeGeneres. DeGeneres has welcomed McKinnon on her talk show multiple times, and one of McKinnon's best known impressions is of DeGeneres.

Okay to Be Gay

Fortunately, in the past few decades, more gay and lesbian comedians have felt comforable coming out, which has paved the way for people like McKinnon to be accepted in mainstream culture. While working on *The Big Gay Sketch Show*, McKinnon met comedian Julie Goldman, who was like an older sister to her.

McKinnon was also able to work with Rosie O'Donnell, a pioneer for lesbian comedians. When O'Donnell officially came out in 2002, she had a successful talk show and magazine and was a household name. She became an activist for gay rights, a voice for LGBT individuals across the country. McKinnon told After Ellen, "These are people who have made it OK for me to be gay, to be who I am right now, and I'm just so grateful as a person to them for their work and what they've done for all of us."

Today, having LGBT characters and actors in television shows and movies is more common than

Rosie O'Donnell came out as a lesbian in a time when being a part of the LGBT community could ruin a person's career in entertainment. However, she continued working as an actress, talk show host, and activist.

it has ever been. Lesbian actresses—such as Lea DeLaria, star of *Orange Is the New Black*—have more opportunities to act in lesbian roles than before. DeLaria had been on the comedy scene since the 1980s and was the first openly gay comic to be on a late-night television show. DeLaria is very open about her sexuality. She has often advocated for an LGBT person's right to come out when and to whomever they felt comfortable with. Though she has been working as an entertainer for decades, it was not until *Orange Is the New Black* premiered in 2013 that she became a household name, bringing LGBT humor and issues to mainstream America.

TRAILBLAZING ELLEN

Ellen DeGeneres was born near New Orleans, Louisiana, in 1958. In the 1970s, DeGeneres began performing stand-up in small venues, such as coffeehouses, which led to gigs around the country in comedy clubs. By 1982, Showtime had named her the Funniest Person of the Year. Her hit show, *Ellen*, started in 1994. DeGeneres came out in a *TIME* article and on her show. *Ellen* became one of

Ellen DeGeneres, host of her own long-running talk show, has been an inspiration to young LGBT entertainers. She is shown here at the 2017 MTV Video Music Awards.

the first shows to really advocate for gay rights and the first with an LGBT main character.

In 2003, Ellen's daytime talk show, *The Ellen DeGeneres Show*, went on the air. It is one of the most successful and longest running talk shows in America. Ellen won the Mark Twain Prize for American Humor in 2012. In 2016, President Barack Obama awarded DeGeneres the highest civilian honor in the United States: the Presidential Medal of Freedom.

A Voice for the Future

Even so, there is still room for improvement in show business when it comes to casting and writing LGBT characters. When Jen Yamato of Daily Beast asked Paul Feig if Kate McKinnon's character in the movie was gay, he replied, "What do you think?" He would not officially confirm or deny if it were the case. He continued, "I hate to be coy about it. But when you're dealing with the studios and that kind of thing ..." Moments like this show that there is still prejudice out there, both in the United States and across the world. Studio executives believe that if a character is going to appeal to "everyone," then they should not be outwardly gay.

Many directors worry about writing an LGBT character into a mainstream movie or show because it is a high risk. What if it is rejected in foreign countries that are not accepting of homosexuality? What if it does not appeal to more conservative viewers? Sarah Kay Ellis, the CEO of GLAAD (Gay and Lesbian Alliance Against Defamation), says this lack of LGBT portrayal in media is harmful. In the 2016 GLAAD Studio Responsibility Index report, Ellis wrote, "Leaving LGBT people out of the picture — or including them only as a punchline — keeps old prejudices alive and creates an unsafe environment, not only here in America, but around the world where most audiences see these depictions."

This is why Kate McKinnon's work is so important. The more roles she plays—the greater her audience—the more she will normalize her sexuality in mainstream media. She told the Logo television network, "I don't want to be a straight girl in movies. I want to be doing what I want and using who I am, authentically."

McKinnon is a continuation of strong lesbian comics who have come before her—Danitra Vance, Ellen DeGeneres, Rosie O'Donnell, and Lea DeLaria. However, she is also a voice for the future. She takes the hardships and tragedies of being a minority, of being on the fringe, and transforms them into something hopeful. She told After Ellen, "I think the best comedy is grounded in true, utter tragedy—and also profound hope."

CHAPTER SEVEN

The Future of Comedy Is Female

Kate McKinnon is just one of the many female comedians who are changing the script in the world of comedy. For a long time, comedy was dominated by men. Most comedy movies starred men, from *Monty Python and the Holy Grail* to *Young Frankenstein* to the original *Ghostbusters*. As shown by the negative reactions some people had to a female *Ghostbusters* reboot, some men are still against women in comedy. Thanks to trailblazing comediennes, however, the world of comedy is becoming more equal each year.

Comediennes in History

For much of history, women have been kept off the stage—unless they are playing a damsel in distress, a sidekick, or a love interest. From the

Lucille Ball broke barriers in comedy with her famous television show *I Love Lucy*.

late 1800s to the 1930s, vaudeville was a popular form of entertainment in the United States. This musical comedy show involved dancing, singing, acrobats, and comedians. Women got involved but rarely had the chance to steal the show.

All of that changed in the 1950s. Female comedians such as Phyllis Diller, Joan Rivers, Lucille Ball, and Carol Burnett broke onto the scene. Phyllis Diller performed her first stand-up routine in 1955. She was a housewife and mother who found her voice on the stage, making people laugh about life in the suburbs with her dry humor. She performed on a game show hosted by comedian Groucho Marx and became a celebrity.

Lucille Ball is often best known for her role on the television show *I Love Lucy*. It followed the marriage between Lucy and her husband. Her costar on the show was Desi Arnaz, her actual husband. Together, they created not only an Emmy Award–winning show, but a booming business: Desilu Productions. The Lucille Ball Desi Arnaz Museum in her hometown of Jamestown, New York, became the National Comedy Center. It is advertised as the first state-of-the-art museum to celebrate the story of comedy in the United States.

THE VARIETY QUEEN

Carol Burnett is widely regarded as a pioneer in the world of comedy. Born in 1933 in San Antonio, Texas, she had a natural talent for acting and making people laugh. In her early twenties, she began performing her own acts and in variety show acts alongside famous comedians, such as Ed Sullivan. Burnett was also a Broadway star, known for her role as Princess Winifred the Woebegone in *Once Upon a Mattress*, both on stage and in the Disney movie adaptation.

Despite success in other genres, variety shows were Burnett's passion. In 1959, Burnett joined a variety show called *The Gary Moore Show*. Variety shows, like vaudeville, contain separate performances within one larger show, often

Carol Burnett is a giant in the history of comediennes. As a well-rounded entertainer, she was famous for her acting, comedy, and hosting skills.

including music, dances, skits, and acting. Like Kate McKinnon, Carol Burnett had a knack for creating characters with personalities so big they could steal the show. She also performed as part of Lucille Ball's variety show *The Lucy Show*. However, it was Burnett's big dream to be the star of her own variety show. So, in 1967, she created *The Carol Burnett Show*, a game-changer in the world of comedy. The show rain for eleven seasons and won more than twenty Emmys.

Saturday Night Live Flips the Script

Saturday Night Live created a new venue for female comedians to show what they could do. In fact, comedian Gilda Radner was the first person Lorne Michaels hired for the show in 1975. Candice Bergen was the first woman to host *SNL* that same year. Jane Curtin was the first woman to host the Weekend Update segment of the show. Years later, Curtin admitted that some of her costars did not think women were funny, and it was a challenge to work there as a woman. The show was a groundbreaking comedy phenomenon, but it still had a long way to go.

Over time, *SNL* worked toward more equal casting, and more women were able to show their talent. Amy Poehler and Tina Fey both had their big break on the show. In 1999, Tina Fey became the first female head writer for *SNL*. In 2004, Fey and Poehler became an unstoppable pair when they became the hosts of Weekend Update, and each woman's comedy career has only continued to grow since then.

The Future of Comedy

By the time Kate McKinnon joined the cast of *SNL*, it was clear that women could lead in comedy. Her success is built upon the women who came before her, from Carol Burnett to Tina Fey. As the first openly lesbian cast member of *SNL*, she has broken the glass ceiling yet again and carved out a place for more women to move ahead.

McKinnon's involvement in the female reboot of *Ghostbusters* also highlighted her belief that women can be as funny as men. McKinnon told David Grove of We Got This Covered:

> Along with being asked to join *Saturday Night Live*, this, getting this role, was the biggest thing that has ever happened in my career. When I heard that Paul Feig was directing an all-female *Ghostbusters*, I was prepared to do anything to be a part of this, to be a part of what sounded like an incredible project.

McKinnon's specific style of comedy also means that she is able to blur the lines between male and female. She is open to playing male characters, as seen in her impersonations of Justin Bieber and Jeff Sessions. Her *Ghostbusters* character Jillian Holtzmann has a masculine quality about her. McKinnon is able to bring her signature style and comedic touch to all of her characters—regardless of sex—which gives her a huge range.

In many ways, McKinnon represents the future of comedy. She has proven herself as a comedic force in movies, on stage, and on the most popular sketch show in America. When an important new role must be played on *SNL*, it is often McKinnon who takes it—proving that she is a frontrunner of the show and can hold her own. Her openness about her sexual orientation will undoubtedly pave the way for other LGBT performers to make their way into mainstream culture. She is bold, unapologetic, and, most important, herself.

McKinnon, the Master

How did Kate McKinnon go from Long Island theater kid to one of the most famous comic voices in America? As her story shows, it took a lot of work, determination, and a passion for making people laugh.

It seems McKinnon always has a new project in the works, from voice acting to shooting a new movie, and she is always growing in her talents. Perhaps it is because McKinnon knows the value of hard work. She told Hunt and O'Connell of *Hollywood Reporter*, "I'm just so tired. And I just prayed for so many years to be tired because I was just so unemployed and had so much time, and was just so desperate to be working like a dog, and now I *am* for the moment." It is clear that McKinnon is grateful for the work she has—and she is not going anywhere.

McKinnon has demonstrated that she can perform at all levels, from stand-up comedy

McKinnon is shown here posing with her second-straight Emmy Award statue at the 2017 Emmy Awards in Los Angeles.

to huge Hollywood movies. She can perform musically, write sketches, and impersonate anyone. As the only *SNL* cast member to win two Emmys in a row, she has stolen the stage and the hearts of people across America and the world. She continues to prove—through her authenticity, hilarity, and range—that she is a comedy master.

Fact Sheet on Kate McKinnon

Full name: Kathryn McKinnon Berthold
Birthplace: Sea Cliff, Long Island, New York
Birth date: January 6, 1984
Parents: Michael Berthold (architect), Laura Campbell (social worker)
Siblings: Emily Lynne Berthold (comedian)
College attended: Columbia University
Occupation: Comedian, actress
Marital status: Single
Children: A cat named Nino
Current residence: New York, New York
Mentors: Julie Goldman, Rosie O'Donnell, Ellen DeGeneres, Lorne Michaels
Career if she wasn't a comedian: A carpenter who lives in the woods
Her first job: An umpire at little league softball games
One thing she's really good at: Cooking

Fact Sheet on Kate McKinnon's Work

Comedy Troupes

The Varsity Show
Upright Citizens Brigade

Sketch Teams

High Treason
Beneath Gristedes
Tremendous Machine
Gramps

Solo Shows

Disenchantment
Best Actress
Kate McKinnon on Ice

Film

2010 *Mr. Ross*, Debby
2011 *Elizabeth Taylor's Video Will*, Elizabeth Taylor
2011 *Pudding Face*, Amy
2012 *My Best Day*, Heather
2012 *Hannah Has a Ho-Phase*, Nicky
2014 *Life Partners*, Trace
2014 *Balls Out*, Vicky
2015 *Giant Sloth*, Nina (voice)
2015 *Ted 2*, herself
2015 *Staten Island Summer*, Mrs. Bandini Jr.
2015 *Sisters*, Sam

2016 *The Angry Birds Movie*, Stella/Eva (voice)
2016 *Finding Dory*, Stan's Wife (voice)
2016 *Ghostbusters: Answer the Call*, Dr. Jillian Holtzmann
2016 *Masterminds*, Jandice
2016 *Office Christmas Party*, Mary Winetoss
2017 *Rough Night*, Pippa
2017 *Leap!*, Regine Le Haut / Felicie's Mother
2017 *Ferdinand*, Lupe (voice)
2018 *Irreplaceable You*, Glass Half Full Kate
2018 *Family*, Jill
2018 *The Spy Who Dumped Me*, Morgan Freeman

Television

2007–2010 *The Big Gay Sketch Show*, multiple episodes, multiple characters
2008 *Mayne Street*, "Parking Tickets," Olga Svenson
2010 *We Have to Stop Now,* "Celesbianism," Angela
2010 *Concierge: The Series*, multiple episodes, Mary
2010 *Vag Magazine*, multiple episodes, Bethany
2010–2011 *Robotomy*, multiple episodes, multiple characters (voice)
2010–2016 *The Venture Bros.*, multiple episodes, multiple characters (voice)
2011 *The Back Room*, "Todd Barry," Susan Boyle
2011 *The 40-Year-Old 20-Year-Old*, multiple episodes, various characters
2012–present *Saturday Night Live*, multiple episodes, multiple characters

2013 *Toy Story of Terror!*, PEZ Cat (voice)
2013 *Hudson Valley Ballers*, multiple episodes, Just Jamie
2014 *Comedy Bang! Bang!*, "Nick Offerman Wears a Green Flannel Shirt & Brown Boots," Effie Villalopolus
2014–2015 *The Awesomes*, multiple episodes, multiple characters (voice)
2015 *China, IL*, multiple episodes, Sunshine (voice)
2015 *The Spoils Before Dying*, "That's Jazz," Dallas Boudreaux
2015 *Difficult People*, "Pledge Week," Abra Cadouglas
2015 *Moonbeam City*, "Lasers and Liars," Panache Miller (voice)
2015–2016 *Family Guy*, multiple episodes, multiple characters (voice)
2015–present *Nature Cat*, multiple episodes, Squeeks (voice)
2016 *Maya & Marty*, "Jimmy Fallon & Miley Cyrus," Heidi Cruz
2016 *The Simpsons*, "Gal of Constant Sorrow," Hettie (voice)
2017 *Friends from College*, "All-Nighter," Shawna
2017–present *The Magic School Bus Rides Again*, multiple episodes, Fiona Felicity Frizzle (voice)
2018 *Sesame Street*, "Elmo's Nursery Rhyme," Mother Goose

Video Game Credits

2015 *Lego Dimensions*, Dr. Jillian Holtzmann (voice)

Famous Impersonations

Hillary Clinton
Ellen DeGeneres
Justin Bieber
Ruth Bader Ginsburg
Jeff Sessions
Kellyanne Conway

Sketch Characters

Fitzwilliam (*The Big Gay Sketch Show*)
Olya Povlatsky (*Saturday Night Live*)
Mrs. Rafferty (*Saturday Night Live*)
Barbara DeDrew (*Saturday Night Live*)

Awards

2014 American Comedy Awards, Winner for Best Comedy Supporting Actress–TV for *Saturday Night Live*

2016 Winner of the Critics' Choice TV Award for Best Actress in a Comedy Series for *Saturday Night Live*

2016 Primetime Emmy, Winner for Outstanding Supporting Actress in a Comedy Series for *Saturday Night Live*

2016 Women Film Critics Circle Awards, Winner for Best Comedic Actress for *Ghostbusters*

2017 Primetime Emmy, Winner for Outstanding Supporting Actress in a Comedy Series for *Saturday Night Live*

2017 Gay and Lesbian Entertainment Critics Association, Winner of the Dorian Award for TV Musical Performance of the Year for *Saturday Night Live*

2018 Gay and Lesbian Entertainment Critics Association, Winner of the Dorian Award for TV Musical Performance of the Year for *Saturday Night Live*

2018 Winner of the CinemaCon Award for Comedy Star of the Year

Critical Reviews

Kate McKinnon on Ice

"If Kate McKinnon's peers aren't quietly jealous of her, they should be. In her third and latest solo show of sketches and characters, *Kate McKinnon on Ice*, she hits her stride and proves to be a rarity: a hilarious physical actor whose is also smart and funny enough to write for herself."—Jane Borden, *Time Out New York*

Ghostbusters

"No one performance dominates the new *Ghostbusters*, which is for the most part democratically comic (a Paul Feig signature), although Kate McKinnon's magnificent, eccentric turn comes close … Here, she embodies the new 'Ghostbusters' at its best: Girls rule, women are funny, get over it."—Manohla Dargis, *New York Times*

"McKinnon's Holtzmann is the straw that stirs the drink throughout *Ghostbusters*, her performance one that easily could have been an exercise in phoned-in snark, but instead proves to be an example of genuinely smart, specific and confoundingly funny characterization."—Ann Hornaday, *Washington Post*

Saturday Night Live

"In three minutes, McKinnon's 'Hallelujah' brought into focus a broken nation, a search for answers and a yearning for change, while at the same time paying tribute to the recent passing of legendary Canadian artist Leonard Cohen who wrote the song. It wasn't funny. It was perfect."—Andree Lau, Huffington Post *Canada*

The Spy Who Dumped Me

"The key to her marvelously uninhibited performance, repurposing a technique she has deployed on *Saturday Night Live* and elsewhere, is that she treats Morgan's international-woman-of-mystery dreams as they deserve to be treated, as both completely serious and utterly ridiculous."
—Justin Chang, *Los Angeles Times*

Timeline

January 6, 1984 Kate McKinnon is born.

2002 Kate McKinnon graduates from North Shore High School.

2006 Kate McKinnon graduates from Columbia University with a degree in theater.

2007 Kate McKinnon makes her debut on *The Big Gay Sketch Show* as a regular cast member.

2008 Kate McKinnon begins performing with the Upright Citizens Brigade in New York City.

2009 Kate McKinnon wins the Logo NewNowNext award for Best Rising Comic.

2012 Kate McKinnon joins the cast of *Saturday Night Live.*

2014 Kate McKinnon wins an American Comedy Award.

2015 Kate McKinnon begins playing Hillary Clinton as she runs for president of the United States in the 2016 election.

October 3, 2015 Kate McKinnon plays alongside Hillary Clinton in a sketch on *Saturday Night Live*.

2015 Kate McKinnon stars alongside her sister Emily Lynne in the web series *Notary Publix*.

2016 Kate McKinnon stars in *Ghostbusters: Answer the Call* with fellow *Saturday Night Live* comedians Leslie Jones and Kristen Wiig, as well as Melissa McCarthy.

2016 Kate McKinnon wins an Emmy for Outstanding Supporting Actress in a Comedy Series.

November 12, 2016 Kate McKinnon performs "Hallelujah" on the cold open after the 2016 presidential election, an iconic moment in *Saturday Night Live* history.

2017 Kate McKinnon voice-acts the part of Lupe in the animated movie *Ferdinand*.

2018 *The Spy Who Dumped Me* starring Mila Kunis and Kate McKinnon premieres.

Glossary

advocate One who defends a cause or other people.

astrophysics A branch of astronomy dealing especially with the behavior, physical properties, and processes of space objects and happenings.

authenticity True to one's own personality, spirit, or character.

collaboration A project or task in which people work together.

comedienne A female comedian.

dialogue A conversation between two or more people.

dyslexia A learning disability involving difficulties in acquiring and processing language.

electoral college A body of electors that elects the president and vice president of the United States.

elicit To draw forth or bring out.

encourage To inspire someone to do something.

exposure The condition of being made known.

feminist A person who believes in and fights for political, economic, and social equality of the sexes.

genesis The coming into being of something.

GLAAD The Gay and Lesbian Alliance Against Defamation. A media monitoring organization established by LGBT people in the media.

humanize To represent someone or something as human or sympathetic.

hypothesize To make an educated guess about something.

impersonate To assume or act the character of.

impression An imitation of someone.

improvise To create something offhand, or in the moment.

inauguration A ceremony to take political office.

incorporate To blend into something.

interview A meeting to obtain information.

introvert A shy or reserved person who likes to spend time alone.

lesbian A woman who is sexually attracted to other women.

minority A part of a population differing from others in some characteristics and often subjected to differential treatment.

misogyny The hatred of women.

persona A character assumed by an actor.

progressive Interested in new ideas, findings, or opportunities.

ridicule To make fun of.

satire A creative work that makes fun of people or things.

sexual orientation The inclination of an individual with respect to heterosexual, homosexual, and bisexual behavior.

significant Important.

troupe A group of theatrical performers.

versatile Having a variety of talents, skills, or uses.

For More Information

Canadian Improv Showcase
2 Amberglen Court
Holland Landing, ON L9N 1J6
Canada
905-967-0141
Website: http://www.canadianimprovshowcase.com
Canadian Improv Showcase is a short-form improv troupe that showcases Canadian humor into interactive comedy.

Canadian Organization of Stand-Up Comedians1300 Gerrard Street East
Toronto, ON M4L 1Y7
Canada
Website: http://canadianstandup.ca
Facebook, Twitter, and Instagram: @canadianstandup
The Canadian Organization of Stand-Up Comedians is an organization that unifies the voices of stand-up comedians across Canada.

Ladies of Comedy Association
Website: https://www.theladiesofcomedy.com
Twitter: @ladiesofcomedy
This networking organization connects female executives in the comedy industry to advance the careers and positions of women in comedy.

National Comedy Center
203 West Second Street

Jamestown, NY 14701
(716) 484-2222
Website: https://comedycenter.org/lucy-desi-museum
Facebook: @nationalcomedycenter
Twitter and Instagram: @ntlcomedycenter
The National Comedy Center is a museum dedicated to the history and future of comedy in the United States.

Upright Citizens Brigade
153 East 3rd St
New York, NY 10009
(212) 366-9231
Wesbite: https://ucbtheatre.com
Facebook, Twitter, and Instagram: @UCBComedy
The Upright Citizens Brigade has theaters and comedy classes around the country.

Women in ComedyChicago, IL
(773) 231-8035
Website: https://www.womenincomedy.org
Facebook: @ladiesincomedy
Twitter: @women_in_comedy
Instagram: @womenincomedy
Women in Comedy is a nonprofit organization dedicated to educating, empowering, and connecting female comedians.

For Further Reading

Belge, Kathy, and Marke Bieschke. *Queer: The Ultimate LGBT Guide for Teens*. Minneapolis, MN: Quarto Publishing Group, 2018.

Bent, Mike. *The Everything Guide to Comedy Writing*. Cincinnati, OH: F+W Media, 2010.

Besser, Matt. *The Upright Citizens Brigade Comedy Improvisation Manual.* Vancouver, Canada: University of British Columbia Press, 2017.

Clinton, Hillary Rodham. *What Happened*. New York, NY: Simon and Schuster, 2018.

DeGeneres, Ellen. *Seriously … I'm Kidding*. New York, NY: Grand Central Publishing, 2012.

Hill, Doug, and Jeff Weingrad. *Saturday Night: A Backstage History of Saturday Night Live*. Untreed Reads, 2011.

Hines, Will. *How to Be the Greatest Improviser on Earth*. Pretty Great Publishing, 2016.

Horner, William T, and M. Heather Carver. *Saturday Night Live and the 1976 Presidential Election: A New Voice Enters Campaign Politics.* Jefferson, NC: McFarland and Company, Inc, 2018.

Huegal, Kelly. *LGBTQ:* The Survival Guide for Lesbian, Gay, Bisexual, Transgender, and Questioning Teens. Minneapolis, MN: Free Spirit Publishing, 2018.

Kaplan, Steve. *The Hidden Tools of Comedy: The Serious Business of Being Funny.* Studio City, CA: Michael Wiese Productions, 2013.

Kirwood, Tony. *How to Write Comedy: Discover the Building Blocks of Sketches, Jokes and Sitcoms—and Make Them Work.* London, UK: Robinson, 2014.

Kohen, Yael. *We Killed: The Rise of Women in American Comedy*. New York, NY: Picador/ Farrar, Straus and Giroux, 2013.

Mardell, Ashley. *The ABC's of LGBT+*. Coral Gables, FL: Mango Media, 2016.

Miller, James Andrew, and Tom Shales. *Live From New York*. New York, NY: Back Bay Books, 2015.

Mizejewski, Linda, Victoria Sturtevant, and Kathleen Roe. *Hysterical!: Women in American Comedy.* Austin, TX: Austin University of Texas Press, 2017.

Napier, Mick. *Improvise: Scene from the Inside Out.* Denver, CO: Meriwether Publishing, 2015.

Perret, Gene. *Comedy Writing Self-Taught: The Professional Skill-Building Course in Writing Stand-Up, Sketch, and Situation Comedy*. Fresno, CA: Linden Publishing, 2015.

Poehler, Amy. *Yes Please.* New York, NY: Dey Street Books, 2015.

Randazzo, Joe. *Funny on Purpose: The Definitive Guide to an Unpredictable Career in Comedy*. San Francisco, CA: Chronicle Books, 2014.

Rosenfield, Stephen. *Mastering Stand-Up: The Complete Guide to Becoming a Successful Comedian.* Chicago, IL: Chicago Review Press Incorporated, 2018.

Shatz, Mark, and Melvin Helitzer. *Comedy Writing Secrets: The Best-Selling Guide to Writing Funny and Getting Paid for It*. Cincinnati, OH: Writer's Digest Books, 2016.

Thompson, Kelly. *Ghostbusters: Answer The Call.* San Diego, CA: IDW Publishing, 2018.

Toplyn, Joe. *Comedy Writing for Late-Night TV: How to Write Monologue Jokes, Desk Pieces, Sketches, Parodies, Audience Pieces, Remotes, and Other Short-Form Comedy*. Rye, NY: Twenty Lane Media, 2014.

Tropiano, Stephen. *Saturday Night Live FAQ: Everything Left to Know About Television's Longest Running Comedy.* Milwaukee, WI: Applause Theatre & Cinema Books, 2014.

Wassan, Sam. *Improv Nation: How We Made a Great American Art.* Boston, MA: Mariner Books, 2018.

Bibliography

Anolik, Lili. "How S.N.L.'s Kate McKinnon Became Comedy's Brightest Star." *Vanity Fair*, September 27, 2017. http://www.vanityfair.com/hollywood/2017/09/kate-mckinnon-cover-story.

Biography.com. "Kate McKinnon." Retrieved August 31, 2018. http://www.biography.com/people/kate-mckinnon-21241425.

Bonner, Mehera. "The Funniest Sketches from SNL's Funniest Women." *Marie Claire*, February 14, 2015. http://www.marieclaire.com/culture/news/a13359/snl-40-funniest-women-sketches-of-all-time.

Bradley, Laura. "Why Saturday Night Live's Bill Hader Got Booted from Kate McKinnon's Audition." *Vanity Fair*, March 13, 2018. http://www.vanityfair.com/hollywood/2018/03/bill-hader-snl-kate-mckinnon-audition-ellen-degeneres.

Chen, Joyce. "Ruth Bader Ginsburg on #MeToo, Kate McKinnon's 'SNL' Impression." *Rolling Stone*, June 25, 2018. http://www.rollingstone.com/tv/tv-news/ruth-bader-ginsburg-on-metoo-kate-mckinnons-snl-impression-127689.

Columbia University School of the Arts. "Theatre." Retrieved August 31, 2018. http://arts.columbia.edu/theatre-arts.

Dunphy, Rachel. "McKinnon, CC '06, SNL Comedienne, Receives Varsity Show's Diamond Award." *Columbia Daily Spectator*, May 6, 2013. http://www.columbiaspectator.com/2013/05/06/mckinnon-cc-06-snl-comedienne-receives-varsity-shows-diamond-award.

The Ellen DeGeneres Show, featuring Bill Hader, 2018 (TV).

The Ellen DeGeneres Show, featuring Kate McKinnon, 2016 (TV).

Flayton, Leigh. "Kate McKinnon & Her Sister Had the Funniest Childhood." Refinery29, May 14, 2015. https://www.refinery29.com/2015/05/87355/kate-mckinnon-interview-sister-saturday-night-live.

Gallagher, Brenden. "The 25 Most Famous UCB Alumni." *Complex*, February 26, 2013. http://www.complex.com/pop-culture/2013/02/the-25-most-famous-ucb-alumni.

GLAAD. "Home." Retrieved August 31, 2018. http://www.glaad.org.

Grove, David. "Exclusive Interview: Kate McKinnon Talks Ghostbusters." We Got This Covered. Retrieved October 20, 2018. https://wegotthiscovered.com/movies/exclusive-interview-kate-mckinnon-talks-ghostbusters.

Howard, Adam. "How 'Saturday Night Live' Has Shaped Our Politics." NBC News, September

3, 2016. http://www.nbcnews.com/pop-culture/tv/how-saturday-night-live-has-shaped-american-politics-n656716.

Hunt, Stacey Wilson, and Michael O'Connell. "Lena Dunham, Amy Schumer and Comedy Actress A-List in Raunchy, R-Rated Roundtable." *Hollywood Reporter*, May 27, 2015. https://www.hollywoodreporter.com/features/lena-dunham-amy-schumer-comedy-797861.

IMDb. "Kate McKinnon-Awards." Retrieved August 31, 2018. http://www.imdb.com/name/nm0571952/awards.

Itzkoff, Dave. "Kate McKinnon on 'Ghostbusters,' 'S.N.L.' and Hillary Clinton." *New York Times*, May 9, 2018. http://www.nytimes.com/2016/08/04/movies/kate-mckinnon-on-ghostbusters-snl-and-hillary-clinton.html.

Kuczynski, Alex. "She's Out Of the Closet. Now What?" *New York Times.* March 3, 2002. http://www.nytimes.com/2002/03/03/style/she-s-out-of-the-closet-now-what.html.

Morris, Alex. "How Kate McKinnon Became the 'SNL' Weirdo-in-Chief." *Rolling Stone*, June 25, 2018. http://www.rollingstone.com/tv/tv-features/how-kate-mckinnon-became-the-snl-weirdo-in-chief-192554.

Morrow, Brendan. "Kate McKinnon's Family: 5 Fast Facts You Need to Know." Heavy, June 16, 2017.

https://heavy.com/entertainment/2017/06/kate-mckinnon-family-mother-father-sister-laura-michael-emily-lynne.

Rosa, Christopher. "16 Times Women Changed the Game on 'Saturday Night Live'." *Glamour Magazine*, June 27, 2018. http://www.glamour.com/story/history-of-women-on-saturday-night-live.

Saturday Night Live, featuring Dave Chappelle, 2016 (TV).

Saturday Night Live. NBC. Retrieved August 31, 2018. http://www.nbc.com/saturday-night-live.

Shuster, Yelena. "One Funny Voice at a Time." *Columbia College Today*, 2007. http://www.college.columbia.edu/cct_archive/mar_apr07/features2.html.

UCBComedy. "Kate McKinnon." Retrieved August 31, 2018. http://www.ucbcomedy.com/user/9402.

UCB Theatre. "Kate McKinnon on Ice." Retrieved August 31, 2018. http://www.ucbtheatre.com/show/2738.

Varsity Show, The. "Home." Retrieved October 12, 2018. http://www.thevarsityshow.com.

Wallace, Amy. "Kate McKinnon Is Comedy's Not-So-Secret Weapon." *GQ*, May 21, 2018. http://www.gq.com/story/kate-mckinnon-profile-2018.

Watkins, Gwynne. "Kate McKinnon on Channeling Her Inner Goat for 'Ferdinand'." Yahoo! News, December 7, 2017. http://www.yahoo.com/entertainment/kate-mckinnon-channeling-inner-goat-ferdinand-191448506.html.

Yamato, Jen. "'Ghostbusters' Director Paul Feig on the Film's Misogynistic Trolls: 'It's Not for All These Guys!'" Daily Beast, July 12, 2016. https://www.thedailybeast.com/ghostbusters-director-paul-feig-on-the-films-misogynistic-trolls-its-not-for-all-these-guys.

Yua, Jada. "Who Ya Gonna Troll?" *Vulture*. Retrieved December 18, 2018. https://www.vulture.com/2016/07/paul-feig-ghostbusters-reboot-c-v-r.html

Index

About the Author

C. R. McKay is an author and editor who has written numerous fiction and nonfiction books for children and young adults. She lives for stories, libraries, and ice cream. She lives in Buffalo, New York, with her husband and two crazy rescue animals. She watches *Saturday Night Live* every chance she gets—as long as she can stay awake for it.

Photo Credits

Cover, p. 3 David Livingston/Getty Images; cover background, interior pages (curtain) Kostsov/Shutterstock.com; p. 7 DFree/Shutterstock.com; p. 11 IFA Film/United Archives/Newscom; p. 13 Everett Collection, Inc./Alamy Stock Photo; p. 17 NBC Television/Archive Photos/Getty Images p. 18 Bruce Yuanyue Bi/Lonely Planet Images/Getty Images; p. 24 Tribune Content Agency LLC/Alamy Stock Photo; p. 27 Daniel Zuchnik/FilmMagic/Getty Images; p. 29 Ron Galella/Ron Galella Collection/Getty Images; p. 31 Anthony Behar/Sipa USA/AP Images; p. 35 Jeff Kravitz/FilmMagic, Inc/Getty Images; p. 37 JB Lacroix/WireImage/Getty Images; p. 39 Pixplus/Bauer-Griffin/GC Images/Getty Images; p. 41 Alex Wong/Getty Images; p. 46 Owen Franken/Corbis Historical/Getty Images; p. 48 Jared Siskin/Patrick McMullan/Getty Images; p. 51 Paul J. Richards/AFP/Getty Images; p. 55 Aaron P. Bernstein/Getty Images; p. 58 Kathy Hutchins/Shutterstock.com; p. 59 United Archives GmbH/Alamy Stock Photo; pp. 65, 79 Pictorial Press Ltd /Alamy Stock Photo; p. 68 Michael Ochs Archives/Moviepix/Getty Images; p. 73 Tommaso Boddi/Getty Images; p. 75 Kevin Mazur/WireImage/Getty Images; p. 81 Courtesy Everett Collection; p. 85 Jason LaVeris/FilmMagic/Getty Images.

Design and Layout: Nicole Russo-Duca; Editor: Siyavush Saidian; Photo Researcher: Sherri Jackson